THE
FUTURE
OF WORK

HOW TO SURVIVE
AUTOMATION AND AI

ASH MASHHADI

*This book is dedicated
to my family.*

The future is yours.

First published in Great Britain by Design Inspiration Publishing
inspiration.co.uk

Designed and typeset by Ash Mashhadi
Cover designed by Ash Mashhadi

ISBN 9798388212078

Contents

V. Thriving in the Future of Work   41

VI. Transferable Skills   51

VII. The Future of Hiring and Firing   59

VIII. What Does it all Mean?   67

"The working environment of the future will be a place of great opportunity and challenge, where old jobs fade away like the morning mist, and new ones arise. Those who can adapt and upskill will thrive, while those who resist will be left behind, wondering what happened."

Are you ready to embrace the winds of change?

Introduction:

I.

Welcome to the Future of Work

Introduction:

I.

Welcome to the Future of Work

The Changing Nature of Work in the Digital Age

The world of work is undergoing a transformation of seismic proportions, with technological advancements and globalization reshaping the way we live and work. From the rise of remote work, to the gig economy, to the increasing use of automation and artificial intelligence, it can be challenging to keep up with the changing landscape and adapt to the new normal of work.

The Future of Work: How to Survive Automation and AI is a book that aims to help you navigate and thrive in this new environment. It explores the benefits and challenges of remote work, the opportunities of the gig economy, and automation. It offers practical advice and strategies for adapting and succeeding in the digital age.

Remote work in particular, has become increasingly popular due to the proliferation of digital tools and the COVID-19 pandemic. Whilst working remotely has its benefits, such as increased flexibility and the ability to work from anywhere, it also brings its own set of challenges, such as the need for strong communication and self-motivation. In this book, we will delve into the best practices for successful remote work, including setting up a functional home office, maintaining work-life balance, and staying connected with colleagues.

The gig economy, which refers to the increasing trend of short-term or freelance work, has also had a major impact on the way we work. While gig work can offer greater flexibility and the ability to choose your own projects, it also comes with its own set of challenges, such as the lack of job security and benefits.

In this book, we will discuss the pros and cons of gig work and offer strategies for succeeding in the gig economy. Including strategies such as building a strong personal brand, networking effectively, and managing finances.

Adapt to Survive and Thrive in the Future of Work

It is no surprise that automation and the increasing use of artificial intelligence in the workplace are changing the job market and the skills that are in demand. In this book, we explore the impact of automation on the job market and discuss the skills and abilities that will be most in demand in the future. Skills such as problem-solving, critical thinking, and collaboration. Abilities such as learning to use AI tools to your advantage rather being at their mercy. This book will also offer strategies for upskilling and reskilling to stay competitive in the face of automation. Strategies such as identifying areas for growth and learning, and taking advantage of online resources and training opportunities.

Who is This Book For?

Whether you are an employee looking to build a successful career in the digital age, a staff manager, or a business owner seeking to stay competitive in a rapidly evolving market, *The Future of Work: How to Survive Automation and AI* will provide you with tools and insights you need to navigate the new normal of work and succeed in the digital age.

Maybe your job was or will soon be threatened by the changes wrought by the new technology. Whatever your situation, this book has been written to help you take control of your life.

This book has been split into chapters and sections based around each of the key issues. This means you are in control of how you read it. You can start and finish pretty much anywhere. The order in which you choose to read it is entirely up to you. You can even leave out the bits that you are less interested and jump straight to the sections that interest you most. If you prefer to eat your dessert first, that's fine.

Whichever way you choose read it, this book is full of useful information, insights and advice for anybody who is hoping to survive and even thrive the workplaces of the future.

About the Author

Ash Mashhadi has been involved in the digital economy since the late 1980s when "graphical user interface" was the hot new phrase. He started a successful digital design agency 1993 which continues to adapt and take advantage of every new wave in technology. Ash has worked as a designer, SEO consultant, and business mentor. Today, he writes books for entrepreneurs and anyone seeking success.

He has been at the practical end of digital design and business for three decades and has learned that in an industry where change is constant, the ability to predict what's coming around the corner is crucial.

Automation and artificial intelligence are transforming the global work environment. Nearly all of us will be affected to a greater or lesser degree over the coming decades, so we all need to equip ourselves adequately if we hope to survive, let alone thrive.

Ash's mission is to help you deal with the changes that new technology brings. That's why this book is your best guide to the future of work.

II.
The Rise of Remote Work

II.
The Rise of Remote Work

The Benefits and Challenges of Remote Work

Remote work, also known as telecommuting, working from home, or hybrid working, has become increasingly popular due to the proliferation of digital tools and the COVID-19 pandemic. The percentage of people working remotely at least part of the time has jumped dramatically. Between 2019 and 2021, the number of people primarily working from home in the US tripled from around 9 million people to 27.6 million people, according to an American Community Survey.

There are many benefits to remote work, including increased flexibility, the ability to work from anywhere, and potential cost savings for both employees and employers.

For employees, remote work allows for a better work-life balance and the ability to avoid the daily commute. It can also allow for a more comfortable and personalized work environment as employees have the freedom to set up their work space according to their preferences. It can suit parents of young children, disabled employees, and the neuro-diverse.

For employers, remote work can lead to increased productivity, as employees may have fewer distractions and the ability to tailor their work environment to their needs. Employers may also be able to tap into a wider pool of talent by offering remote work options, as they are not limited to hiring candidates who live in close proximity to the office. Remote work can also lead to cost savings for employers, as they may not need to provide office space and other amenities for remote employees.

However, remote work also comes with its own set of challenges. It can be difficult to stay motivated and focused when working from home, and there may be a lack of separation between work and personal life.

Communication can also be more difficult when team members are not physically present, and it can be harder to foster a sense of community and collaboration. It is also important to consider the potential social isolation that can come with remote work, as employees may not have the same opportunities for in-person interaction with colleagues. In addition, remote workers may face technical challenges, such as issues with internet connectivity or the need for reliable hardware and software.

Tips for Successful Remote Work

To succeed as a remote worker, it is important to set up a functional home office, establish clear communication channels and boundaries, and maintain a healthy work-life balance.

This may involve setting regular work hours, being disciplined about taking breaks, and setting aside some dedicated work space that is separate from your domestic activities.

This can be difficult if space is limited at home. Try to find somewhere that is not in use through the day by family members. If that is impossible, try to negotiate a space (and time) when family members are not allowed to use that space. During the pandemic, many people were forced to work from home, and at first this became quite a difficult issue in many homes. Eventually, most managed to find a routine or arrangement that worked, so plan this carefully if you are going to be working from home for extended periods.

It is also important to stay connected with colleagues and make an effort to foster a sense of community, whether through virtual team-building activities or regular video conference calls.

Some businesses are already aware of this and arrange frequent opportunities for remote working members of staff to socialize with their office-based employees.

Smart employers that adopt measures like this to encourage team building will earn all the other benefits that come with an inclusive attitude. Employers that only see hybrid working as a way to save money and exploit their workforce will not fare well for long in the new marketplace. Short-term thinking never works for long in business.

It is important for both employees and employers to be proactive in addressing any technical issues or challenges that may arise. With the right tools and strategies, remote work can be a highly effective and rewarding way to work.

Remote work has become increasingly popular in recent years, with many organizations adopting flexible work arrangements and a growing number of professionals choosing to work remotely.

Here are some more tips for anyone that needs to get themselves set up for working from home:

Establish a routine and create a dedicated workspace.
Having a set schedule and a dedicated workspace can help you stay focused and productive when working remotely. It is also important to set boundaries and communicate with your team about your availability. It cannot be good for your mental health to be available 24/7 for work. Make it absolutely clear when you are working and when you are not. Loose arrangements can lead to problems for both employee and employer.

Stay connected and communicate regularly.
One of the challenges of remote work is the potential for feeling isolated. Isolation and loneliness can be a common problem or

freelancers and remote workers of every kind. To combat it, try to stay connected and maintain strong communications with your team and community when you can. Make use of video conferencing tools and regularly check in with your team mates. If that is not enough, look for ways to find social connections outside of the work environment. Apps like Meet-up are great for finding people in your local area that share your interests.

Stay organized and prioritize

The distractions of home life can potentially lead to more disruption than in an office setting. It is important to stay organized and prioritize tasks to ensure that you are productive and efficient. Tools such as to-do lists, scheduling apps, collaboration platforms, and project management software can help you stay organized.

Take breaks and manage your time effectively

Working remotely can sometimes lead to marathon work days and a blurring of boundaries between work and personal life. Working for long periods without sufficient and regular breaks can be harmful to your health and make it difficult to work at an optimum level. It is important to take breaks and manage your time effectively to avoid burnout.

Stay up-to-date with technology and tools

Working remotely often requires the use of a variety of digital tools and technologies. Scheduling apps for social media allow you to save time and effort. AI tools can help you compose content and create graphics for your employers or clients. Staying up-to-date with the latest tools and technologies and being open to learning new ones will ensure that you are able to work effectively and efficiently.

Whether you are new to remote work or an experienced professional, these strategies will help you stay productive, connected, and engaged whether working from home or elsewhere.

III.
The Gig Economy

III.
The Gig Economy

What is the Gig Economy and How Does it Work?

The gig economy is a labor market characterized by the prevalence of short-term contracts or freelance work, as opposed to permanent, full-time employment. The gig economy is often associated with the proliferation of platforms and apps that connect workers with clients or customers, such as ride-sharing, food delivery apps, or home-sharing platforms.

One of the main benefits of the gig economy is the flexibility it offers to workers. Gig work allows individuals to choose when and where they work, and to take on projects that align with their skills and interests. This can be particularly appealing for those who value autonomy and the ability to set their own schedules.

The gig economy also offers a range of opportunities for businesses and organizations. By using gig workers, companies can access specialized skills and expertise on a project-by-project basis, rather than hiring full-time employees. This can be a cost-effective way to access the talent and resources they need, while also giving them the flexibility to scale up or down as needed.

However, the gig economy is not without its challenges. Gig workers often lack the benefits and protections afforded to full-time employees, such as health insurance, retirement plans, and paid time off. In addition, the gig economy can be unpredictable, with gig workers facing the risk of sporadic or inconsistent income. Gig workers usually don't enjoy many of the protections and benefits of traditional employees, but as a trend the gig economy is growing and looks set to remain a key part of the nature of work in the future.

Overall, the gig economy is a complex and rapidly evolving labor market, with both opportunities and challenges for workers and businesses. As it continues to grow and evolve, it is crucial for individuals and organizations to adapt and navigate this new way of work.

Pros and Cons of Gig Work

There are many benefits to remote work, including increased flexibility, the ability to work from anywhere, and potential cost savings for both employees and employers.

For employees, remote work allows for a better work-life balance and the ability to avoid the daily commute. It can also allow for a more comfortable and personalized work environment, as employees have the freedom to set up their work space according to their preferences.

For employers, remote work can lead to increased productivity, as employees may have fewer distractions and the ability to tailor their work environment to their needs. Employers may also be able to tap into a wider pool of talent by offering remote work options, as they are not limited to hiring candidates who live in close proximity to the office. Remote work can also lead to cost savings for employers, as they may not need to provide office space and other amenities for remote employees.

However, remote work also comes with its own set of challenges. It can be difficult to stay motivated and focused when working from home, and there may be a lack of separation between work and personal life.

Communication can also be more difficult when team members are not physically present, and it can be harder to foster a sense of community and collaboration. It is also important to consider the potential social isolation that can come with remote work, as employees may not have the same opportunities for in-person interaction with colleagues.

That's not all, remote workers may face technical challenges, such as issues with internet connectivity and the need for reliable hardware and software. This can have economic as well as technical implications.

How to Succeed in the Gig Economy

To succeed in remote work you will need to master a host of new skills. It is important to set up a functional home office, establish clear communication channels and boundaries, and maintain work-life balance. If you're looking for success in the gig economy, there are eight specific actions you could take:

1. Identify your strengths and skills
The first step to success in the gig economy is figuring out what you have to offer. What are you good at? What skills do you have that are in demand? Consider taking an online skills assessment or asking friends and colleagues for feedback to help you identify your strengths.

2. Choose the right gig platform
There are many gig platforms out there, each with its own unique focus and target audience. Choose one that aligns with your skills and goals. Some popular options have included Uber, Upwork, and Fiverr.

3. Build a strong online presence
In the gig economy, your online presence is key. This includes not only your profiles on gig platforms, but also your personal website and social media accounts. Make sure to present yourself professionally, highlighting your skills and experience.

4. Create a clear and compelling pitch

When applying for gig work, you'll need to convince potential clients that you're the right person for the job. A clear and compelling pitch that showcases your strengths and relevant experience can go a long way towards helping you land work.

5. Stay organized and manage your time effectively

In the gig economy, you'll often be juggling multiple projects at once. It's important to stay organized and manage your time effectively in order to meet deadlines and keep clients happy. Consider using project management tools like Trello or Asana to help you stay on top of tasks.

6. Build a strong network

The gig economy can be a lonely place, so it's important to build a network of other professionals you can rely on for support and advice. Join online communities, attend events and meetups, and consider joining a co-working space to help you connect with others in your field.

7. Be professional and reliable

In the gig economy, your reputation is everything. Make sure to always deliver high-quality work on time and communicate effectively with clients. If you make a mistake, be upfront about it and work to resolve the issue to the best of your ability.

8. Keep learning and growing

The gig economy is constantly evolving, so it's important to stay up-to-date with industry trends and continue learning and growing your skills. Think about taking online courses or workshops to keep your skills sharp and stay competitive.

By following these tips, you'll be well on your way to success in the gig economy. Remember to stay focused, be persistent, and always strive to deliver your best work. With the right tools and strategies, remote work can be a highly effective and rewarding way to work.

IV.
Automation and the Future of Jobs

IV.
Automation and the Future of Jobs

The Impact of Automation on the Job Market

It can't be denied. Automation and artificial intelligence (AI) are already transforming the job market and changing the skills that are in demand. This is having an effect on workforces and businesses across the globe. In this chapter we'll be looking at this more directly.

But first, some quick definitions for the sake of clarity.

Automation refers to the use of technology to perform tasks that were previously performed by humans, while AI refers to the development of computer systems that can mimic human intelligence and perform tasks such as decision-making and problem-solving.

The use of automation and AI in the workplace can lead to increased efficiency and cost savings for businesses, but it also has the potential to displace certain jobs and change the skills that are in demand. It is true that this can be devastating, but it can also provide opportunities for both individuals and businesses.

While some jobs may be automated, others may require new or different skills to take advantage of the capabilities of AI.

For example, the use of automation in manufacturing has led to the displacement of certain jobs, but it has also created new job opportunities in fields such as programming and data analysis.

Jobs That Are Most Likely to be Affected

Some jobs or sectors are more likely to be affected by automation and AI than others. Take a look here and if your job is listed, you need to start making the changes that will help you survive and thrive the future of work.

1. Data entry clerks
2. Customer service representatives
3. Manufacturing workers
4. Retail salespersons
5. Office clerks
6. Bookkeeping, accounting, and auditing clerks
7. Delivery drivers
8. Cashiers
9. Postal workers
10. Data analysts
11. Assembly line workers
12. Bank tellers
13. Telemarketers
14. Travel agents
15. Insurance underwriters
16. Material recorders
17. Watch repairers
18. Textile machine setters, operators, and tenders
19. New accounts clerks
20. Sewing machine operators
21. Weighers, measurers, checkers, and samplers-recorders
22. Sorters, separators, and inspectors
23. Insurance claims and policy processing clerks
24. Procurement clerks
25. Molding, coremaking, and casting machine setters, operators, and tenders
26. Shoe machine operators and tenders
27. Gas compressor and gas pumping station operators

28. Dental laboratory technicians
29. Extruding and drawing machine setters, operators, and tenders
30. Nursing assistants
31. File clerks
32. Library assistants, clerical
33. Medical records and health information technicians
34. Cargo and freight agents
35. Credit analysts
36. Mathematical science occupations, all other
37. Insurance appraisers, auto damage
38. Sewing machine operators, garment
39. Farm labor contractors
40. Medical and health services managers
41. Medical and public health social workers
42. Insurance underwriters, tax
43. Credit authorizers, checkers, and clerks
44. Tax examiners and collectors, and revenue agents
45. Medical transcriptionists
46. Survey researchers
47. Insurance claims clerks
48. Credit counselors and loan officers
49. Payroll and timekeeping clerks
50. Court, municipal, and license clerks

Remember that this list is not exhaustive and the extent to which these and other jobs will be impacted by automation and AI will depend on a variety of factors, including the specific tasks involved in the job and the extent to which those tasks can be automated.

The Role of AI in the Workplace

To succeed in the age of automation and AI, it's important to continuously upskill and reskill to stay competitive in the job market. This may involve identifying areas for growth and learning, and taking advantage of online resources and training opportunities in those areas. It is also important to focus on developing skills that are difficult to automate, such as problem-solving, critical thinking, and collaboration. These skills, often referred to as "human skills", are in high demand in many industries and will be among the ones that are most sought-after in the future.

In addition to upskilling and reskilling, it is important to stay informed about the latest developments in automation and AI and how they may impact your industry or job soon or even further into the future. This may involve reading industry publications, attending conferences or workshops, and networking with professionals in your field. By staying informed and keeping an open mind about new technologies and their potential applications, you can position yourself to take advantage of new opportunities as they arise.

It is also important to recognize that automation and AI are not a threat to all jobs, and they may even create new job opportunities. For example, the development of self-driving cars has the potential to displace certain jobs in the transportation industry, but it also opens up new opportunities in fields such as programming and data analysis.

Rather than viewing automation and AI as a threat, it is possible to embrace them as tools that can enhance and augment the work we do.

The Skills That Will be Most in Demand in the Future

As automation and artificial intelligence continue to transform the job market, certain skills that were once considered unusual or niche may become increasingly desirable to recruiters. Virtual reality design, for example, is an emerging field that involves creating immersive virtual experiences through the use of 3D models and interactive environments. With the rise of virtual and augmented reality technology, there will be a growing demand for professionals who are skilled in this area.

Similarly, work that involves getting the most out of AI could be in high demand. New roles, such as prompt engineering could require creative language skills and could grow in complexity as AI becomes increasingly embedded into our everyday systems. Writing prompts for art generating AI could become more and more sophisticated in future, requiring specialised skill and experience.

Emotional intelligence is a uniquely human key skill that may be in high demand in the future. This involves the ability to understand and manage your own emotions, as well as the emotions of others. As automation and AI take over tasks that are more routine and predictable, there will be a growing demand for skills that are purely human, such as navigating the nuances of human emotions. It is likely to be a very long time before AI is able to accurately read and respond to the ebb and flow of human emotion, so Emotional Intelligence is important for a variety of roles, including leadership, customer service, and sales.

Cultural competency is another important skill that may be in high demand in the future. With the increasing globalization of the job market, there will be a growing demand for professionals who are able to navigate and work effectively in diverse environments. This may involve understanding different cultural norms, communication styles, and ways of doing business. That will still require a human for a while.

By staying up-to-date with the latest trends and developments in your field and continuously learning and adapting, you can position yourself to take advantage of new and unusual skill sets that may arise and be in high demand in the future.

Strategies for Upskilling and Reskilling

Here are some strategies for upskilling and reskilling in the face of automation:

Identify areas for growth and learning
To stay competitive in the face of automation, it is important to continuously learn and grow. This may involve identifying areas of your current role that can be enhanced through additional training or education, or exploring new skills or industries that may be in demand in the future.

Take advantage of online resources and training opportunities

There are a wide range of resources and training opportunities available online, from free MOOCs (massive open online courses) to paid certifications and degree programs. By taking advantage of these resources, you can learn new skills and knowledge at your own pace and on your own terms.

Embrace new technologies as tools to enhance your work

Automation and AI can be used to augment and enhance the work we do, rather than replacing it. By embracing new technologies as tools to improve efficiency and productivity, you can position yourself to take advantage of new opportunities and stay competitive in the job market.

Focus on developing skills that are difficult to automate

In addition to technical skills, it is important to focus on developing human skills such as problem-solving, critical thinking, and collaboration. Creativity is an area where AI is weakest.

Whilst chat-based AI can generate thousands of words of synthesised content, they find it impossible creating new, original work. Humans are still the only ones capable of doing that. Similarly, AI art is still only a synthetic blend of art styles that have previously been created by humans. There is no true originality involved yet.

Originality and creativity are difficult to program and automate, yet they are in high demand in many industries. Until they can be programmed, only humans own the ability to truly create.

New Roles That Are Likely to be Created

Many new jobs and skills will be in demand in the future, to a greater or lesser degree. Only time will tell us where most of the opportunities will lie. The fans of automation tell us that the opportunities created by AI will be infinite. Though that may be a little idealistic, there will be new jobs created by AI. Here is a short list of some potential new roles that are likely to be in demand in the future. Take a look and see if any of them are areas in which you could become adept.

1. AI developers and engineers:
These professionals will be responsible for designing, building, and maintaining AI systems and applications.

2. AI researchers:
These professionals will conduct research to advance the field of AI and develop new algorithms and techniques.

3. AI project managers:
These are the people who will be responsible for managing AI projects from conception to deployment, including coordinating teams, budgets, and timelines.

4. AI trainers:
These professionals will be responsible for training AI systems and algorithms, using large datasets to improve their performance. Eventually, systems will train systems with increasingly complexity, but for a while at least, human intervention will be required.

5. AI ethicists:
These professionals will be responsible for considering the ethical implications of AI systems and applications, and helping to ensure that they are developed and used responsibly.

6. AI sales and marketing professionals:
These professionals will be responsible for promoting AI products and services to potential customers, and helping to establish the AI industry as a whole.

7. AI educators:
As the effects of automation continue to grow more and more individuals will be needed to teach others about AI and its potential uses, including in classrooms and through online courses.

8. AI system administrators:
These professionals will be responsible for the day-to-day maintenance and operation of AI systems, including monitoring

performance, troubleshooting issues, and making updates as needed.

9. AI data scientists:
These professionals will be responsible for analyzing large datasets to identify trends and patterns, and using this data to inform the development of AI systems and applications.

10. AI customer support:
So long as there are customers, there will always be a need for customer support. We will need people who are responsible for helping customers with questions or issues related to AI products and services. This is not something that can be entirely delegated to AI chatbots.

11. AI content creators:
These professionals will be responsible for creating content related to AI, such as writing articles, creating videos, or designing infographics, to educate and inform the public about the field.

Content creators can have enormous reach and are able to shed light on all the opportunities through their creativity.

12. AI product managers:
These professionals will be responsible for defining the features and functionality of AI products, and working with development teams to bring these products to market.

13. AI legal professionals:
These professionals will be responsible for understanding the legal implications of AI and helping to ensure that AI systems and applications are developed and used in a way that is compliant with relevant laws and regulations.

14. AI policy analysts:
These professionals will be responsible for studying the impact of AI on society and developing recommendations for policy makers on how to best regulate and govern the use of AI.

15. AI business analysts:
These professionals will be responsible for analyzing the business impact of AI, including identifying areas where AI could be used to improve efficiency or reduce costs.

16. AI UX/UI designers:
These professionals will be responsible for designing the user experience and user interface for AI products and applications, to make them easy and intuitive to use. The accessibility of AI tools will be crucial in deciding whether they are adopted or not.

17. AI quality assurance professionals:
Quality assurance is vital in order to ensure the best systems are created. These professionals will be responsible for testing AI systems and applications to ensure that they are reliable and working as intended.

18. AI product marketing professionals:
These professionals will be responsible for promoting AI products and services to potential customers, including through marketing campaigns, events, and online channels.

19. AI technical writers:
These professionals will be responsible for creating technical documentation for AI products and services, including user manuals, API documentation, and white papers.

20. AI public relations professionals:
These professionals will be responsible for managing the public image of an AI company or product, including through media relations, social media, and other channels.

21. AI financial analysts:
These professionals will be responsible for analyzing the financial impact of AI, including forecasting revenue and profitability.

22. AI recruiters:
These professionals will be responsible for finding and hiring top talent for AI companies, including identifying and sourcing

candidates with the skills and experience needed for roles in the industry.

23. AI accessibility specialists:

These professionals will be responsible for ensuring that AI products and services are accessible to users with disabilities, including through the use of assistive technologies such as screen readers and speech recognition software.

24. Automation engineers:

As AI is used increasingly in industries across the globe, these professionals will be responsible for designing, building, and maintaining automation systems and applications.

25. Automation project managers:

These professionals will be responsible for managing automation projects from conception to deployment, including coordinating teams, budgets, and timelines.

26. Automation technicians:

These professionals will be responsible for installing, maintaining, and repairing automation equipment. Until we can automate maintenance, this will remain a human task for a long time to come.

27. Automation sales and marketing professionals:

These professionals will be responsible for promoting automation products and services to potential customers. Humans are likely always going to be better able to understand and connect with other humans, and sales and marketing is about understanding and connecting with people.

28. Automation system administrators:

These professionals will be responsible for the day-to-day maintenance and operation of automation systems, including monitoring performance, troubleshooting issues, and making updates as needed.

29. Automation data scientists:

These professionals will be responsible for analyzing data generated by automation systems to identify trends and patterns, and using this data to inform the development of new automation systems.

30. Automation customer support:
These professionals will be responsible for helping customers with questions or issues related to automation products and services.

31. Automation educators:
These professionals will be responsible for teaching others about automation and its potential uses, including in classrooms and through online courses.

This is a crucial role as it will help both future generations and anyone now who's work has been affected by the rising tide of automation and articifical intelligence.

32. Automation legal professionals:
These professionals will be responsible for understanding the legal implications of automation and helping to ensure that automation systems are developed and used in a way that is compliant with relevant laws and regulations.

33. Automation policy analysts:
These professionals will be responsible for studying the impact of automation on society and developing recommendations for policy makers on how to best regulate and govern the use of automation.

34. Automation business analysts:
These professionals will be responsible for analyzing the business impact of automation, including identifying areas where automation could be used to improve efficiency or reduce costs. Businesses, small and large will need to rely on business analysts and consultants who understand the opportunities and impacts that are likely to be wrought by AI.

35. Automation UX/UI designers:
These professionals will be responsible for designing the user experience and user interface for automation products and applications, to make them easy and intuitive to use.

36. Automation quality assurance professionals:

These professionals will be responsible for testing automation systems and applications to ensure that they are reliable and working as intended.

37. Automation translators:

These professionals will be responsible for translating automation-generated text or speech into different languages, to make automation products and services accessible to a global audience.

38. Automation product marketing professionals:

These professionals will be responsible for promoting automation products and services to potential customers, including through marketing campaigns, events, and online channels.

39. Automation technical writers:

These professionals will be responsible for creating technical documentation for automation products and services, including user manuals, API documentation, and white papers.

40. Automation public relations professionals:

These professionals will be responsible for managing the public image of an automation company or product, including through media relations, social media, and other channels.

41. Automation financial analysts:

Similar to the business analysts mentioned above, these individuals will be responsible for analyzing the financial impact of automation, including forecasting revenue and profitability for automation products and services.

42. Automation recruiters:

These professionals will be responsible for finding and hiring top talent for automation companies, including identifying and sourcing candidates with the skills and experience needed for roles in the industry.

43. Automation accessibility specialists:

These professionals will be responsible for ensuring that automation products and services are accessible to users with disabilities, including through the use of assistive technologies such as screen readers and speech recognition software.

44. Automation process improvement specialists:
These professionals will be responsible for identifying ways to streamline and optimize business processes through the use of automation.

45. Automation machine learning engineers:
These professionals will be responsible for developing and implementing machine learning algorithms and models in automation systems.

46. Automation process improvement specialists:
These professionals will be responsible for identifying opportunities to streamline and improve automation processes, and implementing changes to increase efficiency and effectiveness.

47. Automation quality control professionals:
These professionals will be responsible for ensuring that automation systems and processes meet established quality standards and requirements.

Automation will continue to have an enormous impact on the workplace, and it will be increasingly important to ensure that systems work for the benefit of organizations and individuals alike.

48. Automation network administrators:
These professionals will be responsible for managing and maintaining the networks and infrastructure that support automation systems.

49. Automation cybersecurity specialists:
These people are professionals who will be responsible for protecting automation systems and data from cyber threats and vulnerabilities.

This is a role that is important now and will be increasingly crucial over the coming years.

50. Automation logistics professionals:

These professionals will be responsible for managing the flow of goods and materials through automation systems, including tracking inventory, coordinating transportation, and optimizing supply chain operations.

V.
Thriving in the Future of Work

V.
Thriving in the Future of Work

Facing Displacement

If you have suffered redundancy or replacement at work by the rising tide of automation or artificial intelligence, you will know that the effects on your situation, your finances, and your mental health can be quite dramatic. Everyone reacts to change in their own way, so it won't come as a surprise to hear that there is a wide spectrum of these effects.

Here are some of the most common ways being displaced in the workplace by automation and AI can affect people negatively. Bear in mind that this is by no means an exhaustive list, and your own experience may differ, but it is always best to know what the most common experiences are likely to be.

Financial stress and insecurity
Losing a job can be a major financial blow, especially if a person was relying on that income to support themselves or their family.

Loss of professional identity
For many people, their job is a significant part of their identity and sense of purpose. Losing a job can be a devastating blow to a person's sense of self-worth and can lead to feelings of inadequacy or failure.

Difficulties finding new employment

Depending on the local job market and the person's skills and experience, it may be difficult for someone who has been made redundant to find a new job, especially if their previous job has been automated or replaced by artificial intelligence.

Loss of social connections

A person's job can often be a source of social connections, and losing a job can lead to a loss of those connections and a sense of isolation.

Negative impact on mental health

Losing a job can be a major stressor and can lead to a range of negative mental health consequences, including anxiety, depression, and difficulty sleeping.

Disruption to personal and family life

Losing a job can also disrupt a person's personal and family life, including causing strain on relationships and affecting a person's ability to meet their responsibilities and obligations.

Lack of job satisfaction

Even if a person is able to find a new job after being made redundant, it may not be as fulfilling or satisfying as their previous job, leading to feelings of frustration or disappointment.

Decreased job security

The rise of automation and artificial intelligence may lead to a general sense of insecurity about job stability, as people may worry that their jobs could be replaced by technology in the future.

Loss of benefits

A person who loses their job may also lose access to benefits such as health insurance, retirement plans, and other perks, which can have significant financial consequences.

Decreased job opportunities

The increasing use of automation and artificial intelligence may also lead to a decrease in the overall number of job opportunities available, making it more difficult for people to find work.

Difficulty adapting to new technology
Even if a person is able to find a new job after being made redundant, they may have to learn new skills or adapt to new technologies, which can be challenging and time-consuming.

Negative impact on self-esteem
Losing a job can be a major blow to a person's self-esteem, especially if they feel that they have been replaced by technology. This can lead to feelings of inadequacy and self-doubt.

Decreased job mobility
If a person's previous job has been automated or replaced by artificial intelligence, it may be more difficult for them to find similar work in the future, which can limit their job mobility.

Loss of professional development opportunities
A person who loses their job may also lose access to opportunities for professional development, such as training and education, which can impact their future career prospects.

Decreased earning potential
Depending on the nature of the job that has been automated or replaced, a person who loses their job may have difficulty finding comparable work that pays as well, leading to a decrease in their earning potential.

Negative impact on physical health
Losing a job can be a major stressor, and long-term stress has been linked to a range of physical health problems, such as heart disease, high blood pressure, and weakened immune system.

Loss of work-life balance
A person's job can often be a source of structure and routine in their life, and losing a job can disrupt that balance, leading to difficulties in managing other responsibilities and obligations.

Negative impact on family dynamics
Losing a job can also have a ripple effect on a person's family, potentially causing tension and strain within the household.

Difficulty accessing credit

Losing a job can make it more difficult for a person to access credit, as they may no longer have a steady income or may have a lower credit score due to financial strains.

Negative impact on retirement savings

A person who loses their job may also lose access to a retirement savings plan, which can have long-term consequences for their financial security in retirement.

How to Cope

It isn't really within the scope of this book to be a guide to dealing with these effects, our aim is to equip you with strategies to take advantage of the digital revolution at work. However, if you have suffered negative personal effects we encourage you to seek help and guidance from professionals where appropriate.

In addition to professional help, please consider these suggestions as a starting point to helping yourself cope with displacement.

Seek financial assistance

There may be government programs or other resources available to help people who have lost their jobs due to automation or artificial intelligence.

Find support

Connecting with friends, family, or a support group can be helpful in dealing with the emotional fallout of losing a job.

Take care of yourself

It's important to prioritize self-care during this stressful time, including getting enough sleep, eating well, and staying active.

Seek out new job opportunities

Even if the job market is tough, it's important to keep looking for new employment opportunities.

Consider retraining
If a person's previous job has been automated or replaced by artificial intelligence, they may need to consider learning new skills in order to find work in a different field.

Explore entrepreneurship
Losing a job can be an opportunity to explore entrepreneurship and start a business.

Seek out temporary or contract work
In the short-term, taking on temporary or contract work can help provide some financial stability while a person looks for a permanent job.

Find ways to reduce expenses
Losing a job can be a financial strain, so it's important to look for ways to cut costs where possible.

Take time to grieve
It's natural to experience grief after losing a job, and it's important to allow yourself time to process those emotions.

Seek out professional help
If the stress of losing a job is overwhelming, it may be helpful to seek out the support of a mental health professional.

Stay positive
It can be tough, but it's important to try to stay positive and look for the silver lining in difficult situations.

Seek out free or low-cost activities
Losing a job can be a financial strain, so it's important to look for ways to stay entertained and engaged without spending a lot of money.

Connect with others with shared experiences
Hearing from others who have experienced redundancy or replacement at work due to automation or artificial intelligence can be helpful in coping with the challenges.

Find ways to stay productive

Even if you're not working, it's important to find ways to stay engaged and productive, whether that's through volunteering, taking up a hobby, or learning a new skill.

Look for ways to improve your job prospects

This could include updating your resume, networking, or taking on additional training or education.

Find ways to manage stress

Stress is a natural part of the job search process, so it's important to find healthy ways to manage it, such as through exercise, meditation, or talking to a trusted friend or family member.

Stay active

Staying active, whether through exercise or other activities, can help improve mental health and provide a sense of structure and routine.

Stay connected

Losing a job can lead to a sense of isolation, so it's important to stay connected with friends, family, and other social support networks.

Seek out free or low-cost mental health resources

If you're struggling with your mental health, there may be free or low-cost resources available to help you cope.

Seek out career counseling

If you're unsure about what to do next, career counseling can be a helpful resource in exploring your options and finding the right path forward.

Adaptability and Resilience

The importance of adaptability and resilience in the modern workplace cannot be overstated. In today's fast-paced, constantly changing job market, the ability to adapt and bounce back from challenges is key to success.

One of the main drivers of change in the job market has always been new technology. Advances in automation and artificial intelligence (AI) are transforming the way we work and the skills that are in demand.

To stay competitive in this environment, it is important to continuously upgrade your skill set in order to stay current and relevant. This may involve identifying areas for personal and professional growth and learning, and taking advantage of training resources and opportunities to acquire new, relevant skills.

In addition to upskilling and reskilling, it is important to stay informed about the latest developments in your field and how they may impact your industry or job. By staying informed and keeping an open mind about new technologies and their potential applications, you can position yourself to take advantage of new opportunities as they arise.

Adaptability and resilience play an important role in the face of other types of change too, such as shifts in the economy or changes in the workplace. For example, the rise of the gig economy has led to a proliferation of short-term or freelance work, which can be unpredictable and may require a different approach to work and career planning. By being adaptable and resilient, you can navigate these changes and continue to pursue your goals.

In addition to the practical benefits of adaptability and resilience, these skills can also have a positive impact on your mental health and well-being. By embracing change and viewing challenges as opportunities to learn and grow, you can cultivate a sense of resilience and optimism that can help you cope with stress and adversity.

Overall, adaptability and resilience are essential skills in the modern workplace. By continuously learning and adapting, and by staying resilient in the face of change, you can position yourself to thrive in the ever-evolving job market. If only one thing is certain about the future of work, it is that change is likely to be a pivotal feature.

Building a Successful Career in the Digital Age

As we look to the future of work, it is clear that the job market is in a state of flux. The rise of remote work, the growth of the gig economy, automation and AI, and other trends are all contributing to a rapidly changing landscape.

So what does all of this mean for the future of work? It is difficult to predict with certainty, but it is likely that we will see a continuation of many of the trends we are already seeing. Remote work, for example, is likely to become even more prevalent as digital tools and infrastructure improve, and more businesses adopt flexible work arrangements. The gig economy is also likely to continue to grow as more people seek out flexible and on-demand work.

Automation and AI will continue to transform the job market, and it is important for individuals and organizations to stay adaptable and up-to-date with the latest developments in these areas. This may involve continuously upskilling to stay competitive in the job market, and embracing new technologies as tools to enhance and augment the work we do. It is also important to focus on developing skills that are difficult to automate, such as problem-solving, critical thinking, and collaboration, as these skills will be in high demand in many industries.

In addition to technological trends, economic and societal factors will also play a role in shaping the future of work. Economic factors such as globalization and the rise of emerging markets may lead to changes in the demand for certain skills and job roles. Societal factors, such as changing demographics and values, may also influence the way we work and the types of work that are in demand. Also, climate change is likely to continue to be a major cause of displacement and to affect social, economic and political situations both locally and across the globe.

Ultimately, the future of work is likely to be shaped by a complex interplay of these and other factors. By staying informed and adaptable, and by continuously learning and growing, we can position ourselves to thrive in the face of change.

VI.
Transferable Skills

VI.
Transferable Skills

What are Transferable Skills?

Transferable skills are abilities that can be used in a variety of different job roles and industries. They are often skills that are not specific to a particular job or industry, but can be applied to many different types of work.

One example of a transferable skill is effective communication. This skill is important in many different types of jobs, as it allows you to clearly convey your ideas and thoughts to others, whether you are working in a customer service role, a management position, or any other type of job. Effective communication involves being able to listen actively, speak clearly, and write concisely, and it can be valuable in a wide range of job settings.

Another example of a transferable skill is problem-solving. This skill involves being able to identify and analyze problems, generate potential solutions, and choose the best course of action. This skill is important in many different types of jobs, as it allows you to find creative solutions to challenges and to make effective decisions.

There are many other examples of transferable skills, including leadership, time management, teamwork, and adaptability. Skills such as these can be developed through a variety of different experiences, such as education, internships, volunteer work, self-education, and even hobbies.

When job seeking, it is important to highlight your transferable skills on your resume and during the interview process, as they can make you a valuable asset to a wide range of employers.

Why You Need to Identify Your Skills

Transferable skills are abilities that you have acquired through your education, work experience, and personal life that can be applied to a variety of different job roles and industries. These skills are not specific to a particular job or industry, but can be valuable in many different types of work.

Identifying and highlighting your transferable skills can be especially useful when you are looking to change jobs or industries, as it allows you to showcase the abilities and experiences that you have that are applicable to a wide range of different job roles.

There are many different types of transferable skills, and the specific skills that are most valuable to you will depend on your education, work experience, and personal interests. Some common examples of transferable skills include:

Communication
The ability to listen actively, speak clearly, and write concisely can be valuable in many different types of jobs.

Problem-solving
The ability to identify and analyze problems, generate potential solutions, and choose the best course of action can be useful in a wide range of industries.

Leadership
The ability to inspire and motivate others, delegate tasks effectively, and make decisions can be valuable in many different types of work.

Time management
The ability to prioritize tasks, manage your schedule, and meet deadlines can be important in many different job roles.

Teamwork
The ability to work well with others, collaborate, and contribute to a team can be valuable in many different industries.

Adaptability
The ability to adapt to new situations and technologies can be crucial in the rapidly changing world of work.

By identifying your transferable skills and highlighting them in your resume and during the job search process, you can demonstrate to potential employers that you have the abilities and experiences that are valuable in a wide range of different job roles and industries.

This can make you a more competitive job candidate and increase your chances of finding a new job that is a good fit for you.

How to Identify Your Transferable Skills

There are a few basic steps you can take to help you on the journey towards identifying and understanding your own particular set of transferable skills:

Make a list of your education, work experience, and personal interests
Start by making a list of all the education, work experience, and personal interests that you have. This can help you begin to identify the skills that you have acquired through these experiences.

Identify the skills you have used in each of these areas
For each item on your list, think about the specific skills that you have used. These could be skills related to your major or field of study, skills you have developed on the job, or skills you have acquired through hobbies or other personal interests.

Categorize your skills

Once you have identified the skills you have used in each of these areas, try to categorize them into different skill categories. For example, you might have communication skills, problem-solving skills, leadership skills, time management skills, teamwork skills, and adaptability skills.

Reflect on your skills

Take some time to reflect on the skills you have identified and think about how you have used them in different situations. This can help you understand the value of your skills and how they might be applicable to different types of work.

Seek feedback from others

Ask people who know you well, such as friends, family members, colleagues, or mentors, to provide feedback on your skills. They may be able to provide insights into skills that you may have overlooked or undervalued.

Research different job roles and industries

Look into the skills that are required for different types of jobs and industries. This can help you understand what skills are in demand and how your skills might be applicable to different types of work.

Consider your strengths and areas of expertise

Think about what you are particularly good at and what you enjoy doing. These areas of strength and expertise may be transferable skills that you can highlight to potential employers.

Look for patterns in your skills and experiences

Try to identify any patterns in the skills you have acquired and the experiences you have had. This can help you understand what skills you are particularly strong in and how these skills might be applicable to different types of work.

Seek out opportunities to develop your skills

Look for opportunities to develop your skills further, either through education, training, or hands-on experience. This can help you build a stronger foundation of transferable skills that you can draw upon in your job search.

How to Exploit Your Transferable Skills in the Digital Age

Once you have identified your transferable skills, there are a few steps you can take to help you get a job in the future when automation and AI have changed the job market:

Tailor your resume and cover letter

Highlight your transferable skills in your resume and cover letter, and use specific examples to demonstrate how you have used these skills in different situations. This can help you stand out to potential employers and show them how your skills are applicable to the job you are applying for.

Network

Network with people in your industry or in industries that you are interested in. This can help you learn about job openings, get advice and insights from professionals, and make connections that may lead to job opportunities.

Consider further education or training

Consider seeking out additional education or training that can help you develop your skills and knowledge further.

Stay up to date on industry trends

Stay informed about trends and developments in your industry or in industries that you are interested in. This can help you understand what skills are in demand and how you can position yourself as a valuable asset to potential employers.

Be flexible and open to new opportunities

Be open to exploring new opportunities and industries, even if they are outside of your comfort zone. This can help you adapt to changes in the job market and find opportunities that are a good fit for your skills and interests.

Focus on developing in-demand skills

Look into the skills that are most in demand in your industry or in industries that you are interested in, and focus on developing these skills further. This can make you more competitive as a candidate for employment and also increase your chances of finding a job in what is a rapidly changing job market.

Use online tools and resources

Take advantage of online tools and resources, such as job boards, career websites, and professional networking sites, to find job openings and connect with potential employers.

Seek out internships or volunteer work

Consider seeking out internships or volunteer work that can provide you with hands-on experience and help you develop your skills. This can help you build a strong foundation of experience and make you a more competitive job candidate.

Practice your interview skills

Practice your interview skills by rehearsing with friends, family members, or a career coach. This can help you feel more confident and prepared when you are interviewing for jobs.

Be proactive in your job search

Don't wait for job openings to come to you – actively seek out opportunities and reach out to potential employers. This can help you increase your chances of finding a job that is a good fit for your skills and interests.

VII.
The Future of Hiring and Firing

VII.
The Future of Hiring and Firing

How are Automation and AI Changing the Nature of Job Recruitment?

There are many ways that automation and AI are changing the world of job recruitment. If you want to thrive in a future world where automation and AI are crucial parts of the recruitment process, it would be a good idea to acquaint yourself with some of the areas in which this is most likely to occur. How will AI contue to affect the work of recruiters?

Automated resume screening
Many companies are using AI tools to scan resumes and identify candidates who are a good fit for the job. These tools can help companies save time and resources by eliminating the need for a human recruiter to review every resume.

Predictive hiring
Some companies are using machine learning algorithms to predict which candidates are likely to be successful in a given role. This can help recruiters identify top candidates more efficiently.

Virtual interviews
AI-powered virtual assistants are being used to conduct initial job interviews. This can help companies save time and money

by eliminating the need for in-person interviews for the initial screening process.

Recruitment chatbots

Many companies are using chatbots to communicate with job candidates. These bots can answer questions, schedule interviews, and provide information about the company and the job.

Personalized job recommendations

Some job search websites are using AI to recommend job openings to candidates based on their skills, experience, and job preferences. This can help candidates find job openings that are a good fit for them, and it can help companies find candidates who are more likely to be interested in the job and successful in it.

Skills assessment

Some companies are using AI-powered skills assessments to evaluate candidates. These assessments can test candidates' knowledge and abilities in a variety of areas, such as coding, problem-solving, and communication. This can help companies identify candidates who have the skills and abilities needed for a particular job.

Recruitment process automation

AI can also be used to automate certain tasks in the recruitment process, such as scheduling interviews and sending out job offers. This can help companies save time and resources and allow recruiters to focus on more high-level tasks.

Diversity and inclusion

AI can also be used to promote diversity and inclusion in the recruitment process. For example, some companies are using AI to remove names and personal information from resumes in order to reduce bias in the selection process.

Candidate experience

AI can be used to improve the candidate experience by providing personalized communication and support throughout the recruitment process. For example, chatbots can be used to answer questions and provide updates to candidates, and AI-powered virtual assistants can be used to conduct initial interviews.

Remote hiring

The COVID-19 pandemic increased the use of remote work and remote hiring, and AI can be used to facilitate this process. For example, AI-powered video conferencing tools can be used to conduct virtual interviews, and AI-powered skills assessments can be used to evaluate candidates remotely.

Talent sourcing

AI can be used to help companies identify and attract top talent by analyzing data on job candidates and identifying those who are most likely to be a good fit for a particular role. This can be especially useful for companies that are looking to fill specialized or hard-to-fill positions.

Continuous learning

AI can be used to help companies identify and develop the skills of their current employees. For example, AI-powered learning management systems can provide personalized learning paths and recommendations to employees based on their needs and goals. This can help companies upskill their workforce and ensure that they have the skills needed to succeed in an increasingly automated and digitized world.

How to Handle The Changing Nature of Job Recruitment

As AI inevitably infiltrates nearly aspect of the world of work, it it no surprise that recruitment is at the forefront of the adoption of digital assistance. It is only fair that candidates are equipped with some knowledge and tips to deal with it. So here are some detailed instructions on how candidates can prepare for the ways that automation and AI are changing the world of job recruitment:

Automated resume screening

Make sure your resume is optimized for automated resume screening tools. This means using clear, concise language and including keywords related to the job you are applying for. You should also be sure to include all relevant experience and skills, and make sure your resume is free of errors.

Predictive hiring

Research the company you are applying to and the role you are applying for, and try to understand what qualities and skills the company is looking for in a candidate.

This will help you tailor your resume and cover letter to the specific needs of the company and the job.

Virtual interviews

Practice for virtual interviews by doing mock interviews with a friend or family member. Make sure you have a stable internet connection and a quiet, professional-looking space for the interview.

Be sure to test your video conferencing software beforehand to ensure that it is working properly.

Recruitment chatbots

Familiarize yourself with the company and the job you are applying for, as this will help you to ask informed questions of the chatbot and demonstrate your interest in the role.

Personalized job recommendations

Make sure that your job search profiles (such as on LinkedIn) are up to date and accurately reflect your skills, experience, and job preferences.

This will help AI-powered job recommendation systems to accurately match you with relevant job openings.

Skills assessment

Research the skills that are required for the job you are applying for and make sure you have a strong understanding of them. Consider taking online courses or doing other types of training to enhance your skills in these areas.

Recruitment process automation

Keep an eye out for updates or communication from the company throughout the recruitment process. Be sure to respond promptly to any requests or questions, as this will help to keep the process moving smoothly.

Diversity and inclusion

Be aware of the importance of diversity and inclusion in the recruitment process, and be open to discussing these topics with the company.

Candidate experience

Make sure to ask any questions you have about the recruitment process, and be sure to follow up with the company if you haven't heard back from them in a timely manner.

Remote hiring

Familiarize yourself with the video conferencing software that the company is using, and be sure to have a stable internet connection and a professional-looking space for the interview.

Talent sourcing

Keep your job search profiles up to date and be active on professional networking sites like LinkedIn. This will help companies to find you when they are searching for top talent.

Continuous learning

Stay up to date on industry trends and be open to learning new skills. Consider taking online courses or participating in other types of training to enhance your skills and keep them current.

Conclusion:

VIII.
What does it all mean?

VIII.
What does it all mean?

A Rapidly Changing Landscape

The Future of Work: How to Survive Automation and AI has discussed the rapidly changing job market, which is being shaped by trends such as the rise of remote work, the gig economy, and the proliferation of tools using artificial intelligence.

As we have seen, the future of work is a complex and rapidly changing landscape, shaped by a range of technological, economic, and societal factors. From the rise of remote work and the gig economy to the impact of automation and artificial intelligence (AI), the job market is in a state of flux, and it is important for individuals and organizations to stay adaptable and resilient in the face of change.

Disrupting the World of Work

The use of automation and AI in the workplace can lead to increased efficiency and cost savings for businesses, but it also has the potential to displace huge numbers of jobs. The skills that are currently in demand by employers will change both subtly and dramatically. Almost all industries are likely to be affected. If you want to survive or even thrive during this upheaval, you need to acquire new knowledge and skills as quickly as possible.

Continuous Improvement

This has created an environment where, if you want to succeed, it is important than ever to continuously upskill and reskill to stay competitive in the job market. This involves identifying areas for growth and learning and taking advantage of online and offline resources and training opportunities. Sometimes this can involve an investment, but there are often also resources that do not require any financial outlay. Use whatever resources you can find to give yourself an edge.

It is also important to particularly focus on developing those skills that are difficult to automate, such as creative problem-solving, critical thinking, and collaboration. These skills, often referred to as "human skills," are in high demand in many industries, and are hard for software to emulate.

Latest Developments

It will be increasingly important to stay informed about the latest developments in your field and how they may impact your industry or job. By staying informed and keeping an open mind about new technologies and their potential applications, you can position yourself to take advantage of new opportunities as they arise.

This may involve reading industry publications, attending conferences or workshops, and networking with professionals in your field. It can be very time consuming to keep up with all the new developments, but it helps to focus on trying to identify thse which will be key to future changes in your industry.

Adaptability

Adaptability and resilience are also essential skills in the modern workplace. By embracing change and viewing challenges as opportunities to learn and grow, you can cultivate a sense of resilience and optimism that can help you cope with stress and adversity. This is particularly important in today's fast-paced, constantly changing job market, where the ability to adapt and bounce back from challenges is key to success. This may not always seem possible initially, when you have suffered setbacks, but try to treat it as an ongoing behaviour that will benefit you eventually. It can sometimes help to start on a small scale, which you can develop ove time into a healthy habit.

Tech Trends and Societal Change

In addition to technological trends, economic and societal factors will also play a role in shaping the future of work. To thrive in the face of change, it is important to stay informed and adaptable and to continuously learn and grow. Social attitudes towards AI have changed enormously over the years and over time they are likely to fluctuate further. These attitudes will affect our level of adoption and reaction to automation and AI.

Being aware of these attitudes, whether hostile or accepting, must be a crucial part of your toolbox when it comes to understanding the impact of AI in the workplace.

Complexity

The future of work is likely to be shaped by a complex interplay of technological, economic, and societal factors. We don't yet know whether the future of work will be a dystopian hellscape of over-surveilled humans toiling endlessly for a pittance, or a glorious landscape of endless opportunities leading to a human race which no longer needs to struggle for resources and is free to excel.

By staying informed and adaptable, and by continuously learning and growing you can surf the upcoming waves and take advantage of what is coming your way. Make no mistake, these changes are real and substantial. It would not be an exaggeration to describe the shift that is occurring as seismic. Like an earthquake, it is too big to stop, avoid or ignore.

Use this book. Give yourself the edge. For now, and into the future.

By the same author

Nervous about business networking?
This book is for you.

If you dread networking events but have to go anyway, this book is for you. Packed with tips and tactics based on the author's years of experience, this book is the "expert in your pocket" that you need when you network.

This handy guide is full of advice on how to start conversations, how to prepare, spotting who to talk to and who to avoid, how to follow up new connections, and so much more.

"Full of advice that you can use right away!"

Find this book on Amazon now

www.ingramcontent.com/pod-product-compliance
Lightning Source LLC
Chambersburg PA
CBHW070749220526
45467CB00018B/1679